To Vic & Sue
Hope you enjoy
the read

Kian Reland

The Truth behind the Smile

The 2020 Experience

KIAN IRELAND

authorHOUSE®

AuthorHouse™ UK
1663 Liberty Drive
Bloomington, IN 47403 USA
www.authorhouse.co.uk
Phone: UK TFN: 0800 0148641 (Toll Free inside the UK)
       UK Local: 02036 956322 (+44 20 3695 6322 from outside the UK)

Published by AuthorHouse   06/29/2021

ISBN: 978-1-6655-8926-0 (sc)
ISBN: 978-1-6655-8925-3 (hc)
ISBN: 978-1-6655-8927-7 (e)

Print information available on the last page.

Any people depicted in stock imagery provided by Getty Images are models,
and such images are being used for illustrative purposes only.
Certain stock imagery © Getty Images.

This book is printed on acid-free paper.

This book is dedicated to

K.G- the inspiration you have given me in that there are truly amazing people out there.

Kian Brown- my amazing son who has always been an amazing inspiration to me.

Erin Brown – the apple of my eye and off my heart

Those from the social media platform who have looked over me in my darkest days.

Contents

Epigraph

Sometimes going against the grain and standing for what you believe in can bring you the things you desire.

Preface

This book was written in December 2020, during isolation with direct contact with work colleagues as confirmed cases with Covid. Luckily when tested I was not confirmed as having Covid. The strangest circumstances around the book, is that since it was written I have had an incident which resulted in losing my memory and this book is my only link to the year of 2020 as I have lost a huge chunk of the year due to the memory loss. It identifies that some of the events really did happen as I wrote about my life and in an ironic way, I now glad I did as you do not tell everyone everything that happens every day. I owe this story to the people who have contributed to my year and especially those have given me hope in my darkest days.

Chapter 1

A START LIKE NO OTHER

*N*ew Year's Day. Who would have thought going to work on New Year's Day would be a good thing? But for me, working that day was the best option to lift my head and distract myself from the reality of life. I woke up on 1 January 2020 with my marriage on the ropes and no one having a clue about it apart from myself. Walking around work and trying to remain as normal as possible was genuinely easy, aside from the surprised faces of people trying to understand why I was working on New Year's Day. But working was easier than facing the reality of life at home; I was not wanting to face it. So I used work as the perfect setting for escapism. The fear of returning to my home setting was a distant memory for now, with no idea of what was approaching us in 2020.

As January moved on, I took the opportunity to gain another day of escapism from my marriage and went for a walk at one of the UK's most desired locations, but ultimately for the wrong reasons. Beachy Head has always been a beauty spot for me.

· · · · · · · · · ● ○○○○○○○○ ○ ○ ○

On 21 January 2020, I wanted to end my life at Beachy Head and be done with it, but the fear of leaving my kids' lives empty managed to hold me back. And knowing how it had felt losing someone to suicide when I was a kid, I was ashamed of my thoughts and intended behaviour; however, I could not escape the demons in my head and was in search of help. But how and when and with whom could I go about this? First, I needed to do the one thing on that day that completely made sense: confirm the end of my marriage to my wife. So, I went home and told her.

I did not expect the shock on her face. I felt she knew for sure based on circumstances that showed our marriage had been on the slide for some time. How could she not know? Was it complete naivety on her part, or was it all just a complete fantasy in my head? I had been planning this for some time, so it really was nothing new to me; it was a plan six months in the making. At what point had I realised that it was over? We had drifted apart months before, but only in recent reality, as I had started to write my story of where and when we started to drift, that all became real in my head without knowing it. The hardest part was trying to be normal over Christmas 2019 without giving it all away.

The next few weeks were very weird circumstances, living under the same roof as the kids and trying to be as normal as possible while I searched for somewhere else to live. Then there was the reason—well, the believed reason—that my marriage was coming to an end; naturally, it was the very stereotypical belief that a man cheated. In my head, yes, reality-wise, I was interested in someone else, but that was a far cry from the reasons why my marriage failed—quite the opposite. The person I was interested in was probably just the final piece to realising that my marriage could certainly go no further than the current day, hour, minute, and second. So, the marriage ended; it did not come as a shock to my side of the family, but it did shock the other half of the family. The obvious, again stereotypical, view as I entered my fortieth year was this: *Oh, must be having a midlife crisis.*

The two things I was certain of were my marriage was over and it was not ending on the back of a midlife crisis. This ending gave me the opportunity to move on with my life, which I so needed after years of not being happy. And it was not just the marriage I was unhappy about; I had several demons in my head that I needed to put to rest.

The stereotypical, apparent reasoning of why I was leaving was that I was interested in someone else. Yes, I took the heat for our failed marriage. It had become a one-way street, and this was very evident once I revealed the delightful news. I had known the person I was interested in and fond of for some time; it was not just a spur-of-the-moment marriage-rebound scenario, which is just another stereotypical reaction. Being with someone that I wanted to be with had the usual buzz and excitement attached to it, as if suddenly, my life had reversed to times when dating was fun. But at the age of thirty-eight, dating was more of a challenge than just going for a straightforward night out and a few drinks, getting to know each other, and rolling with it. When you enter certain age brackets, you need to overcome completely different hurdles, and some things you do not expect to face.

And so, it began. I asked her out and did not get a reply on the night I asked her. So I had a sleepless night, as if, all of a sudden, I was a teenager putting all his eggs in one basket to date the most gorgeous girl at school. But then, the next morning, I got the reply that I wanted: she did like me. But very much the question loomed: Would we date, or would it still be very much a desire rather than a straightforward "yes, let us do it"?

As the weeks rolled on, it was very much a game of yes–no as she toyed with the idea. At first, I thought it was just nerves, but how we approached it was always going to be complicated. The complications were always things I had expected and prepared myself for. The relationship was very much on one minute and then off the next, which naturally created frustration. But if it were meant to happen, it would.

As the month neared a close, we finally agreed to go for it, with the main obstacle still remaining a challenge. But that obstacle was what had driven the relationship to become a reality. The questions and raised eyebrows from our work colleagues—people we had probably classed as friends once upon a time—certainly played a factor in us getting together, like in a stereotypical happily-ever-after storyline.

The night of 23 January became what sealed our decision to throw complete caution to the wind. And why should we not, being both single and adults? Yes, our being work colleagues was an obstacle, but why is it so doubted that two single colleagues can work together on a professional level and be in a relationship? On that day, we had both been questioned whether we were already dating, which, at that point, we were not. But that inadvertently started our journey together, one that destroyed work friendships, which would never be the same again. Our work friends' approach was again stereotypical and selfish. It never considered any of our actual feelings or circumstances, and it carried a lack of respect for humankind. But the journey began.

We hooked up in a hotel for our first night together. I was slightly nervous on the night; I think we both were quite nervous on the Friday night as we sat in the bar watching *The Masked Singer* on television, a brand-new series where celebrities dressed up in the weirdest of costumes to mask their identity as they sang. Four judges had to try to guess who the celebrities were based on a series of clues. In a sense, we were also aiming to hide our identities from the limelight of dating in public, secluded in a hotel. And unwillingly, this was about to become our lives over the next few months, watching this programme and enjoying a drink and some chips, as we played the game of cat and mouse with each other and with work, which kept our relationship on its radar.

And of course, not to rob you of the most intriguing part, we did make it to my hotel room, like a couple sneaking away to have an affair and have our way with each other tucked away from the glare of suspecting media. It felt like, suddenly, we had become a celebrity couple. It was a nice finish to what had already been a great evening, something I think we both felt we had waited forever to come around.

As we snuggled up and got naked, hot, and steamy, we had sex together, the first time we would sneak around over the coming months. And then suddenly, at the stroke of midnight, it was time for her to leave, as her carriage would be there soon to whisk her back home and aim to avoid the paparazzi as she left, no glass slipper left behind as evidence. As she drove away, I stood in awe and excited like a kid in a candy store at what had finally happened, which we had both craved for some time. And I sparked up a cigarette and took it all in before creeping back to my hotel room to hide away from the media spotlight.

Our first night was blissful, but would it be the start of something amazing in spite of the adversity and challenges of colleagues who date? Or would it mark just another failed opportunity for two people to get together due to the pressures put on them by a frowning society of hypocrites, full of jealousy towards humankind and everyone's right to be happy together?

Chapter 2

REALITY BITES

*A*s January vanished in the midst of excitement and hysteria, trauma, a split marriage, and a new chance to be with someone else, who was fresh, funny, and exciting, I wondered, *Will the relationship last? Will it be what I expect? Will it be more challenging than we expect?* And the reality was that something greater was looming in the background and gripping the world in fear that we were yet to experience. The majority of the world was still living with no concept of what was about to come forward in a great sense of fear, with death and families torn apart.

The month of February arrived. This month normally brings a hysteria of fantasy and happily-ever-afters or flowers and gifts with Valentine's cards expected or craved by those people just wishing for a piece of happiness or excitement. That month, those things would not be on *our* agenda, but we would continue to challenge aspects of dating under the radar, feeling like we were having a secret affair that no one could know about. The next time we met would be at mine, another Friday night of bliss. We had been working together all day, doing visits on her patch and supporting her development. How ironic that I was responsible for her training as a professional and respected person within the business—or was I?

As we stopped off to switch cars, we knew that in a few hours, we would be back together but in a completely different context. Because I had much anticipated her arrival at mine for ages, I cooked for us both—probably about as romantic as I could be in the month of love and hysteria based on traditions that have probably been around since time began. I had even taken the fact that she was vegetarian into consideration, and we both went vegetarian that night. With me being a complete meat eater, that was romantic in the context of the person I was.

So, we tucked into a nice, delicious meal and shared a bottle of wine before snuggling down to watch a movie. I remember the film being *Top Gun*, very cheesy but fitting for what is deemed the most romantic month of the year. It is a film based on a romantic fairy-tale approach: Will the hotshot get the girl? I do not believe we even watched a moment of the film that night as we snuggled up in bed together, gripped in a passionate embrace, and had sex, which was amazing. The foreplay between us was great, as I had planned it out to be a special night, with dinner not the only treat on the menu.

We toyed with and teased each other in a passion that had become a real game between us since I had first revealed my hand. And there I was, with my hands all over her, caressing her neck and touching her intimately as she returned the pleasure. Now, with me getting deep inside her and giving her the ultimate pleasure she craved, we did take a risk that night, going without protection so she could really feel the real pleasure inside her. As we lay back after our immense embrace and snuggled up to settle down for the night, she looked so peaceful lying there, snuggled up with me. Neither of us had a care in the world, apart from the moment that we were enjoying together.

In the morning, when we woke up, we enjoyed another snuggle and had sex again, which was a great thing to wake up to for us both; it capped off what had been an amazing night, and that was breakfast for us both with the most desirable taste. Then, it was very much time to get up, get showered, have a proper breakfast and some tea to get us motivated to leave each other and return to what would appear to be normal life, and go back to playing the game and hiding what we were doing from the world full of critics and hypocrites who can't allow two people to have what they want to experience together.

The ongoing messages and humour between us were immense daily, and we were great work colleagues and great friends. When we were together, we seemed great as a possible couple, which we had never decided on or discussed at any point so far, but we appeared to be naturally heading that way.

The next time we met was our first time together at hers. Our relationship was really getting to be like a secret affair between two married people who sneak off in the night to do the unthinkable under the cover of darkness. The build-up that day had been exciting and created a real buzz of something fresh and new, something I had never experienced on that level before. I got ready that night and drove in my company car to make the fifty-minute journey to hers in what we had joked endlessly about as being *stealth mode* so we could go undetected by many, including those hypocrites at work, her family, and general society. After I parked nearby that evening, I lay in wait for the green light to make the final ten-minute drive to hers with the coast clear. And there it was shortly afterwards, the message to say, "Coast is clear", so I started up the engine and made that drive to hers.

When I parked, I tried to park away from her street and make the approach to her house unnoticed by anyone, as her family lived on the other side of the street. Safe to say, I made it to her door, which she knew was coming. As she opened the door to me, there she was, trying to keep the dog settled to prevent waking up her daughter or shining a light on us in any way, like something out of *Romeo and Juliet*. So, we settled in the front room with a cup of tea and had a quiet laugh and joke together and caught up on how life was in general.

Soon, we made it to her bedroom for the first time for a night of more passionate sex, which did not consist of just doing it once. We both had another great night of pleasure, and soon, with the time passing so quickly, it was 5am. Time to creep back out of the house and into the day, which was still quite dark and gloomy, and vanish before the sun rose on her street. We had the concept in our heads that if the sun rose too quickly, everyone would be standing there in her street, all the hypocrites at work and her family watching me as I left. So up I rose, got dressed, and disappeared after a quick smooch at her front door. I got in my car and raced home before the sun rose, as if the sun could turn me to stone like a vampire. The most amusing part of that night was finding out that her mum had messaged her to say, "Saw a man creeping into your house. Are you okay?"

So, there I was, back in my studio flat, with the thoughts of another great night with someone who was becoming a huge part of my life. But let us not be hasty, as these things can always turn south, and they normally do. The signs were already there on occasion, with the game of cat and mouse very much part of everything. We faced real pressure from those circles of hypocrites who thought we would put all others at risk and who thought they should put the brakes on something going quite well between two people who clearly had a connection and spark between them, which had been a year in the making.

A normal Thursday, and work carried on as it always did, but that would not end well. I got home from work with the normal rush-around routine of getting ready for football training. Thankfully, I was not directly involved; I was more of a coach these days than a player still being put through my paces. But that night, the hypocritical society of so-called friends, colleagues, and those alike was going to put me through my paces.

That evening, I got to the pitches and set up my team of amazing under sevens for another session, alongside my son, who played on the team. But then, my boss rang me to ask me some serious questions. I was like, "You know, I do football training on a Thursday night, and now's not really the time." But persistent as he was, he dropped the question she and I had both been anticipating. Then I knew what was coming, as she and I had already spoken, and I knew someone else had already questioned her. So, step up I did, with my answer of course being, "There is nothing going on between us." My boss had complete cheek to ask that, so I said no. And that was it.

15

I was glad that the conversation was short and sweet, as I was standing next to my son, and that was probably not the best time to be asked that, in his direct earshot. Nevertheless, that conversation was done. And it took me almost a day to compose myself and lay into my boss about it, which I did late on the Friday evening. I gave him a piece of my mind. Yes, respectfully, my dating a colleague should not have been happening, but aside from that, we always remained professional in our job roles and never let our relationship affect our work in any way. So, my message was "Get real and go away, and show more decorum and respect for individuals seeking some happiness together. Your actions are now expected to ruin something built up over time against the many hypocrites and liars." And that they did.

Chapter 3

FLYING SOLO

We exited the month of February—the most romantic month of any year according to the star-crossed lovers seeking something bought, a cheap and tacky gift, for one day a year, which society deems as essential—with me now flying solo again. What would be the approach this time? Would I go it alone or continue to search for that one person who would make the pain of being a single person go away?

The start of this year clearly had not gone to plan. The last time we spent together was a nice evening meal with her and her daughter. Soon, with her daughter in bed, we snuggled up together and got a bit frisky. A bit of oral action ended in an unexpected way as she went cold. With the purest intentions, she just could not do it anymore. I picked her up and moved her off me; she seemed frustrated, which I did not get.

The words came from her mouth as she gestured to the table where, only a few hours before, we all had sat enjoying a meal; she said that held more significance than the passion we shared together. And she was right; of course it did. I never would have got involved with someone who had a child without the knowledge that the child would feature as part of the relationship, as nothing is more important to a mum than her own children. And now, this was clearly over, as she hinted. I should leave but not in a "get out, I do not want you here" way. The reality was that I was probably over the drink limit, so driving right then would not have been the best choice. So, I stayed. We spent our last night together in her bed before separating and going our separate ways. As I crept out at 5am, this relationship was now done—or was it? Back on Single Street it was, and March was here.

How quickly the year had gone already, and everyone was still in need of a wake-up call. A shocking reality not seen in years was about to grip us all, and at a huge scale definitely not experienced in my lifetime. In a year's time,

I would not recall the context of what happened for a large part of the year 2020.

There I was, three months in and starting over for the second time, already seeking to sort out my life again. Time to reconnect with friends, whom we all seem to shut out and do not speak to as much during times when we are with someone, as they always seem to become second best. But when it comes down to it, they always have our backs. So, reconnecting with friends, me making some time for them and them for me, was great. And the shocking reality of what 2020 was to bring was only around the corner.

With the reconnection to friends came some unexpected pressures of life. Why does friendship always seem to come down to what your friends believe is right for you? They deem that your life is built on loneliness based on the situation that you have gone through. I have never had a desire to be lonely, as I always want to be with someone, but I never need to be, as the darkest places we find ourselves in life are the greatest places to find ourselves. Those are where the greatest experiences come from, and we define our lives in these situations. Those are the situations in life that can break us, and to date, they have never broken me long enough to bring my life to a grinding halt. Regardless of how much these periods can be struggles in society, I have found myself repeatedly with each situation add another chink to my armour against a world that can be cruel.

So, with the added pressure of amazing friends who have always been there for me, who have the best intentions for me, I got myself into online dating and became a social media advocate, although I was against it in every sense because of the fantasy society and warped reality that we live in. So, at that point, I chose an option that would work best for me, and that was the key to my latest and continuous period of recovery.

The month of March moved at a rapid speed with little time to breathe, think, and digest the current situation I found myself in. And with bigger things on the agenda right then, I felt life was about finding and focusing on the important things that matter to me, aside from any other external pressures.

In reality, 2020 was about to unexpectedly unleash and shock the world with something, even though the sense was the conspiracy theorists felt this had already gripped the world before we even raised our heads on 23 March 2020. I cannot remember my movements beyond the 23 March 2020 (which to you will become very clear in this book), in the weirdest of circumstances. COVID-19 would bring me the shock that something brave could cause the most damning of darkness but equally create the best circumstances in my life, with a newfound ability. The day 23 March 2020 started as every other day would, but would end with an entire nation left needing answers and leadership, in what would become the largest crisis faced in my lifetime. Many are not old enough to remember the last time when we faced an uncertain future and when the day that we were currently living mattered so much, with the reality of not knowing what we would face tomorrow.

When work finished on that day, I planned to make a trip to her place for dinner with her daughter. So, once I got home from work, I got changed and refreshed for what lay ahead. So now ready, I made the journey to her via the shop to pick up some dinner for us all. I had no ambitions for the night ahead, but would this rekindle something, or would it just be about friendship between two people who held a spark for each other? I arrived with clearly no intentions apart from having a nice dinner with a friend and her daughter—no more, no less—as being friends always holds more value than anything else that two people can share.

That night, we had a nice dinner, all three of us. And as her daughter went to bed, she and I settled down to watch some television and enjoy a good night together as friends. We watched television with the clear knowledge that our prime minister was making some announcement at 9pm. As we watched the announcement, the "stay at home" message came alive for the first time. It all seemed like kind of a laboured reality, but what was going on was still not any clearer. But what did it mean? Would we be cut from society in all aspects? Was it safe to go out? Would we die? Would we see each other again? When would that be? Was this now serious? So many questions! As the announcement ended and the reality set in that, as a nation, we were in trouble, we had no real concept of the future and world that we were now facing. And with that, her phone started, as she was always one step ahead of the crowd.

Despite our friendship, whenever I entered her house, I still discarded my phone like in some undercover operation. We did this purely to avoid any sort of detection, as we live in such a hypocritical society. Those at work could easily track my phone, and would it be so strange to have both our phones in the same location at the same time and at not my address but hers? Then the real questions would start.

I still believed in many concepts those hypocrites at work would end up controlling our lives, as why would they allow anyone to be happy in their life? Were they unhappy in their own lives? (This was clearly the case in this scenario.) I realised at this point in my journey of 2020 that the chats and conversations that led to the rumbling amongst society's hypocrites were clearly laid by one person, with the other ringleader using their manipulative style to throw everyone around them under the bus with contrived stories to save the grace of the original source and to protect the hypocrites who aren't happy in their lives; they need to break a good thing between two people over jealousy. And as it was now very clear that our relationship had come to an end, the hypocrites had won on this occasion, as they always do. The present rumbling of that person was clearly not jealousy that my colleague and I were together (because we weren't by any stretch of the imagination) but jealousy only over the concept that she stood amidst a friendship that the person and I had developed over many years, also as work colleagues. And because I gave more attention to and spent more time with someone else, the friend chose to cause friction by saying to the hypocritical society that my colleague and I clearly had a thing together; this way, the friend could win overall and reclaim their place as the friend and the one who got the attention.

When I got back to my car that night, I was still reeling from the news that our prime minister had just announced. What did it all mean? I stepped into my car and reflected just a minute. As I lit a cigarette and started the engine, I switched on my phone to now alert the hypocrites of society that I was there, and alive, so they could swiftly pick up my scent and location in case they sat there waiting for me to establish my location so they could satisfy themselves that their work was done.

And as that phone came on, there came a constant barrage of messages from my team at work with the who, what, why, and where of COVID! As the messages continued, I literally had to pull over to the roadside and face that conversation, telling them that I knew about as much as they did right then and would update them in the morning once I knew more. And that is how the evening ended, shrouded in controversy, with teams breaking curfew rules and expecting me to instantly have all the answers. If only life was that simple, eh …

Chapter 4

APRIL FOOL'S

*W*hen we all had the news that we were entering lockdown, I again asked myself, *What does that mean?*

On the morning of 24th March, we woke with uncertainty of the road ahead. I opened my laptop after an early morning call, being advised to stay at home for the day; everyone at work would have an update once more was known on our position with work and our road map. So, a conference call happened, and the work began, with the message of staying at home re-enforced and the work beginning. We needed to brief our teams and prepare for the inevitable: that these most unprecedented of times were going to have an impact on our daily lives. We were facing the unknown, as we had entered World War Three overnight. So, we briefed our teams of the changes, and the new workload began, something that would mentally drain us all to the point of exhaustion.

Over the week ahead, we catalogued our teams into sections and tried to identify the risk level for our stores and devise some sort of plan to prepare for the worst. This process was crucial to limiting the risk that this newfound pandemic had unexpectedly shrouded us in. No one was really prepared for this situation.

Once we relayed the message to our stores, it was time to evaluate the risk to our teams and their teams, as everyone was at risk. But at that point, we were very unclear of how the stores would be impacted and what formats would have to steady stores and make them available to trade in the most crucial of times. Overnight, we had gone from a retailer that just existed in a populated market and had no clear identity to one that was better than our competition. We had always been around five to ten years behind our competitors at every turning point. Would this be our chance to step out of the shadows and prove we could lead from the front in a structed manner and give our customers and colleagues a sense of security in the current pandemic circling around with a hugely underestimated threat?

But naturally, we collectively thought about everyone but ourselves, not knowing what impact the days, weeks, and months ahead would have on us and our mental stability. As humans, we tend to do that, or do we? The weirdest of circumstances throw up the weirdest of opportunities. This is a story about living life in 2020 as an individual and the impact it had, something I am sure many of you will relate to in some context. Regardless of how 2020 was for me personally, the pandemic was something that the entire nation felt. So, with the reality on us and the pressure of work thrust into the unknown, we, as a support network to our teams, needed to ensure we looked after ourselves and defined a new way of working that protected us so we offered the best support network that we could.

How do you define a strategy for the unknown? I pondered while I sat looking around my enclosed space consisting of just a room, from which I would have little contact with the outside world over the following months, something I would not appreciate and would take a long time to adapt to. And in the weirdest circumstances, an unexpected lifeline got thrown to me, which seemed like a great thing and gave me a new lease on life for the most challenging times, and which would end something that had been a lifetime in the making.

The lifeline was linked to a case that I had been working on, which was one of the most highly sensitive cases I dealt with in my work. This case shined a light on my colleague and me during our early attempts at dating. It only gave the hypocrites of society ammunition to attempt to separate us and prevent us from getting closer to each other, which seemed to work at the time. Those hypocrites of society balked at the time and effort going into such a high-profile case, which took hours of scrutiny and planning over a period of weeks to put together. And the hypocrites of society circled like vultures, waiting to swoop in and show that they were truly in charge of preventing people from having a life together. It's strange to think that this was a more common exercise than I originally thought.

When you meet someone in life, and you two have something between you, there are always going to be vultures of society and hypocrites determined to bring it down, as they are unsatisfied in their own lives. They choose to prevent others from having any happiness for themselves. Even with the strong connection my colleague and I had between us, work and her training always took priority. I made sure she had the support and training she required to carry out her job to the best of her ability. That responsibility lay in my hands, and I delivered on that time and time again, even though not respected and trusted to do that.

The key element to maintaining good mental health and looking after yourself is developing a structured routine, which you should always do in any sort of crisis, and this pandemic set the biggest challenge we had ever faced, as many of us had never ever experienced anything like it before. I now had my routine down: each morning, I would rise normally, check the latest on the COVID situation with my teams to get an angle on it, and deal with any immediate threat. Then, once I was satisfied that all was under control, I would take an hour to myself to shower or bathe, get dressed, and have a decent breakfast before tackling another day.

The month of April passed by like a sick April Fool's joke cast on society. These days were a challenge, and strongly differing from normal working days, depending on the circumstances. Sometimes, these days might not end until 8pm, as every working moment could very quickly change the operation's demographics. And, in this weirdest world, an opportunity was about to present itself, which I assume the other person totally did not expect. This was all linked to a case that I was involved with at work.

April did cast the weirdest of opportunities on us. Who would have thought that a call with the police would open an opportunity that I do not believe anyone in society would believe in? When I set up the date and time for a call to discuss a recent case to review the evidence and what it meant, it would lead to a chance meeting with someone years after the last meeting I had had with that person. The call brought a least expected reunion in all the chaos.

I set up the call with the police to discuss the case and have the evidence reviewed to see whether any prosecution charges could be taken against the people involved. The meeting to review the evidence lasted around an hour, but something just was not right about it, which did not seem really apparent at the time. As the call carried on, the officer in charge of the case—well, in charge of gathering the evidence, I suppose, and reviewing it for the CPS to see if any charges could be brought against said parties—there seemed to be a certain familiarity about the person, which did not strike me at the time. But we got on with the call anyway. The evidence was reviewed, and then it would go to the CPS to see whether any prosecution charges could be brought.

Once the interview was finished, the officer and I had direct contact because we had each other's numbers, and in the days leading up to the case, we would naturally chat about it and the evidence to see what steps could be taken to bring this to a close. A few days later, on one of the calls, we both approached the question, Do we know each other? I was of the belief that the reality was of course, we did. In fact, we had known each other for so long. And we had unexpectedly found our way back to each other in a bizarre set of circumstances. So, we exchanged private numbers to further our conversations.

Who would have thought a chance meeting was in the pipeline—with someone I had not had any contact with in over thirteen years, since the fateful morning that had seen us go our separate ways? At that point, we had had no plans to meet, but we always had a connection, and was that connection about to spark something that would come to a fairy-tale end? However, now, I faced a trio of strange circumstances. Was I interested in rekindling opportunities that may have already passed me by? The colleague at work who I viewed never as a colleague but as a close friend, after our experiences together, was the one with whom I had a life connection that had been established over time, and a game of yes or no on all the reasons why I would never go back there was circulating in my head.

Then, just to make matters more complicated, I had entered the world of online dating, persuaded to give it a try by friends. And hey, why not? Of course, there was no gain or loss to be had in a world of a new style of dating. I had got to talking online to someone who really seemed quite nice, and again, in circumstance, she also played a role within the police force, a different kind than your everyday position within the police force. Also, as April was nearing a close, the time to move again and start over was drawing closer because my current living situation was not great and space was limited. And I suppose that reality had only become apparent in that month, being confined to a space that was about to get a reality check.

I lived next door to someone very young who was naive in a way in her youth, pure and innocent. We often chatted outside in the night while having a ciggy after she finished her work for the day. One evening while having a ciggy, I was in her proximity for around twenty minutes. Then she dropped the bombshell! "You know I work in a nursing home," she said, as if I had never made that observation in my time living next door to her.

I replied, "Of course I do. How are things up there at present?"

She responded, "Not great. Everyone in my work, including employees, has come down with COVID-19, and I now have to isolate as well as a result!"

There was horror on my face, as that would now describe me, stuck in self-isolation for a period of fourteen days, as if having to roam around in that small place were not bad enough. And I was just in the process of planning to move, which was an unwanted circumstance. The coming fourteen days would be a nightmare for me, always reliant on myself and my own ability. (Even in moments of darkness, you

35

find your greatest moments of brilliance, something that I would heavily realise an exact year from that point in my life.)

In life, there are times when you depend on people, and I cannot give enough thanks to the person who daily delivered me my shopping and kept my sanity intact over the period that seemed to last forever. Without them, I am not sure how I would have found a way to survive. And having my COVID test done in that period proved how unprepared everyone still was for this pandemic at all levels, with results expected back within forty-eight hours but actually received fifteen days later. Waiting fifteen days to receive results that came back as void was about as helpful as being locked inside a fridge with no food to eat!

Chapter 5

MAKING HEADWAY

As I exited the period of self-isolation, I did learn a new ability to cope with a circumstance we all feared in every way: catching COVID-19. COVID-19 was bringing many deaths, and the process had only touched the surface of what lay in front of us. How long would this last? But the period of self-isolation was over for me, for now at least. And I did move out of my current dwelling in May and started over in a new location, one that might bring new challenges, or new happiness. Or would life just continue to be an uphill climb this year that seemed to have no end?

The new place was nice, a distant cry from the studio flat that I had rumbled around in for many months and that had become a real struggle in the past few weeks, being confined to that space, a prisoner of society. This situation was common for a lot of people at present, confined to their locations, some worse than others. Some people had no work available because their employers were forced to close under rules of lockdown, and those with medical conditions were in immediate danger and at high risk of death from COVID-19.

I found myself in a lovely setting in a nice, secluded location, with a nice kitchen, decent-sized bedroom, and good front room. The built-in office layout was clearly the sealing factor in taking on the property; there, I would spend the next few months working from my desk as I managed to get by day by day in COVID-19 and support the outside world from the comfort of my office. And the new place had an escape route as well as a secluded garden down the back where I could settle and relax for escapism from the daily norm as and when it arose.

As May started, it was strange to cave to one of the latest crazes that lockdown had brought in the world of social media. But that month, I would take a step into a world of craziness that would inadvertently shape my future in the way I least expected. I had never been a big fan of social media, but then, after chats with friends, I had decided to take the plunge. And who knew what life experiences it would bring along the way, good or bad? I have always been an upfront and honest person and never had an issue sharing my life experiences, or else I guess I would not be sat here writing this book. And when you join social media, I guess you have the chance to hide behind a profile, being someone you are not or being the person you have always been.

The added anticipation of online dating would also be a factor that month. I was not exactly comfortable with social media, but then, at what point in life do you become comfortable with things? Since the early '90s, the influence of social media and the internet had grown at a massive rate. But much to many people's unknown expectations, lockdown made an app that had been around for years something extremely special.

I connected with someone from online dating, and eventually, we did exchange numbers. She seemed quite nice, but you never know how these things will go. We chatted for some time before arranging to meet up for a date. Clearly, dating in 2020 was not going to be your stereotypical dating, where you simply meet someone you like and hook up with them at a bar, club, or wherever and hope that, in some way, they like you as much as you like them, and you go from there. But 2020 did not permit that, and no doubt, online dating became a more common way of meeting people during 2020. I guess the difference with online dating is that you tend to make more of a connection with someone before dating, while in a world of reality dating, you tend to make the connection afterwards. So, after chatting for a while and exchanging numbers and building some sort of connection between us, we agreed to meet for a date. Choosing locations, of course, was never going to be easy, with us all technically in lockdown, but you do manage to find a way, I guess. We took the steps to arrange to meet at hers, and she arranged to cook us a meal, which was nice.

We had a nice dinner, and afterwards, we settled down to watch a film. It was a nice evening, and we had a connection already based on our conversations while online dating and having message conversations leading up to our first date. We shared some wine, which was nice, and while we watched the film, we made the decision to venture to her bedroom for a while. While in the bedroom, we took the steps to snuggle up together and have passionate sex. She seemed a lot more nervous than I was, but we shared a nice, close embrace. After that, we got dressed and made it back to her front room. Not long afterwards, the night ended, and I disappeared into the night, went back to my car, and returned home to reminisce about our night together.

It was quite the evening and provided quite the escapism for us both in a weird time of life, where I guess dating in person was not permitted—not that the government gave any direct message on dating during lockdown, per se, but it was inadmissible for two people not from the same household to meet. So I suppose the government did not have to put a complete advisory out there that dating was prohibited as part of a national crackdown. But in a world where we crave to take risks, the risk here was limited to just two people trying to make sense of and maybe develop something that could go somewhere in a world of the most challenging scenarios. I stand by the fact that we took those steps against the national lockdown rules as the nation got locked away and lost its freedom of movement.

This connection between us was not one of longevity but one of friendship that still exists, and I am certain it will exist at the time of the release of this book, as we still talk to this day. I recall how nice of a person she really is; in this world of hypocrites and cynics, it is rare to find a good heart in a person. I do recall once while I was working from home, she messaged me to see if I was at home, which I was, and she brought me a coffee before going to collect her daughter from school. This nice surprise proved she had a heart amongst the world of cynics and hypocrites. I do not recall that we dated beyond that moment, but I know that our dating relationship must have ended well, as we still speak.

The month of May moved forward at a sometimes-slow pace, or a fast pace; everyone was unsure of how quickly those days did pass. It was pretty much like being on a revolving hamster wheel or waking up as the lead character in the film *Groundhog Day*. But life did move forward as our nation's people locked themselves away, running around in their hamster wheels, while the government reeled from the effects of COVID-19 and tried to guide us through the current pandemic with not really a clue as to what to do with every step, making catastrophic mistakes time after time, like a group of kids running the country and making every decision based on a game of rock paper scissors. The level of progress that I was making in my own life was based on just going with the flow, but life kept throwing up unexpected paths with every passing day.

I received a message from someone who had been out of my life for years and who I had not expected to hear from, even though we had reconnected by chance just the month before. I responded to her message with no clear objective other than to reply to it. She responded in an unexpected manner, saying we should meet and have a catch-up, as we did not live that far from each other. I agreed and said, "Yeah, that would be nice," but was completely unaware of where it would lead.

A few days later, we did meet up, and had a coffee on the beach and reminisced a bit about times gone by. It had been thirteen years since we last spoke, and here we were, face to face, pondering what could have been or maybe what should have been but for the morning that our relationship came to an end within a matter of minutes. We decided to take the steps to further discuss times past and arranged to meet at mine a few days later for a night of takeaway and wine.

When that night approached, I did not think anything of it or where it would lead, but she arrived in all her finery, dressed to the nines like she was planning to go out for a meal. Of course, that was not strictly going to happen, with the country in a wide crackdown for all functional goings-on.

As the evening grew later, she ended up staying the night and woke up the next morning in my bed—something that was nice and rewarding for us both. But I knew that this was nothing more than maybe nostalgia for a time that once passed us by. I had no real concept of how 2020 was going to change my life in so many ways, as every acquaintance you meet presents opportunities to evaluate situations in your life—something I would not realise the true benefit of until a year later.

And as the month of May started to vanish quicker than it started, the months ahead would really start to add huge life changes in all senses of dramatic change and traumatic change in circumstances and in reality. That was my life all over; it had always been that way. As an individual, you are sometimes powerless to stop such changes from happening, as these moments are what truly shape your life and make you who you are.

Chapter 6

HALFWAY POINT

*A*s I reached the halfway point of the year, with the worst part of the year still ahead, in my head it seemed like things were going to plan, whatever that plan was. The situation with any plan raises this question: How do we plan for the unexpected twists and turns that get thrown at us? We tend to always have a plan B, but can we always have a plan C and beyond?

Social media played a part in my journey, as I made new friends, and we became the "famous six". But would this bring a good outcome or one that would define why social media is an awful, foul place, just like I anticipated when I joined only a month before?

In every group of people, there are always the wannabe leader, the narcissist, the one everyone warms to, the intelligent one, the weak one, and the one who is just there to make up the numbers. We all probably had our reasons for joining a newly growing social media app that was only gaining traction on the back of lockdown. The world probably did not need the app, but it did happen to be there at the time.

With any sort of craze, people tend to jump in without any idea or evaluation of the consequences. So here was a group of six, united in a friendship that would never last, as these things never do. When people are in a group, there is always a tendency for them to try to prove that they are better than everyone else, and we would eventually all split up and go our separate ways in the fight for survival. This newly formed group would very quickly become like we were involved in a lockdown version of *Big Brother*—one that would never see a winner that would result in a huge payday. Was it weird to put trust in these people I did not know? Would it spell some disaster? *Yes* would always be the natural answer to that. But there we were, together in friendship that would barely survive the year due to the nature of the beast.

I felt my role in the group was the comedian, the one who was always up for a laugh and never shied away from humour, which I think is just something that either you have or you simply do not. There were many ups and downs in this insane world of six who had united through social media. Two of the group were obsessed with previous partners and would eventually ditch the group in search of them. In so-called true-friends style, they naturally deserted the group in search of something that had existed prior to the situation they currently found themselves in.

Is always chasing the past tense the key to success and happiness? The answer is no, as once something has come and gone, there is no resurrection, no salvation, no happily-ever-after. Life does not work like that, especially in some social paradox, as naturally, some sort of wound is always left behind between two people in their departure, regardless of time and reason for the divide. So that would leave a group of four remaining, and this you will see later in this story. Friendship can become vicious when the fight for survival starts, and this would be one of shock and awe, but with everything comes life experience, regardless of age.

Back to real-world society now, when my attention returned to her, the one, the connection, the one who should not have been there for many reasons. Once two people go their separate ways, there should be no return, regardless of how right it seems at the time, as you will never install that happiness as it once was. But there we were again, for our second meeting. The truth was that I was always sceptical about our chance meeting. I have always been a strong believer that everything happens for a reason, but I had an inclination that this meeting was not going to end well. I have always had this sixth sense; I had witnessed and felt past experiences before they occurred, and this sixth sense felt stronger than ever. But we did indeed break the value—the rule—that once you have tasted the apple, you do not return there. You leave the apple rotten in the ground and walk away, as it is now poisoned beyond all reasonable doubt, and you poison yourself by going back for another bite.

As human beings, we repeatedly make the same mistakes in life, as it is there that we find solstice and define who we are in life. Reading this, you will probably not quite relate to that point, but you will have a euphoric moment in life that will ultimately define you when it comes. We all believe that things just happen in life, but, in fact, your life is mapped out the minute you are born, and your defining moment can occur when you least expect it.

When you have a connection with someone, regardless of time lapsed, it is rather difficult to leave that apple rotten in the ground; this circumstance or chance in life gives you the urge to taste the forbidden fruit all over again. I enjoyed endless time with the person who had been out of my life for years, but we kept it very low key.

Keeping our relationship low key was vital to us both because we did not want our rekindling to sweep away parties beyond us or to cause them anguish if it went wrong again. And there was a high chance that it would go wrong. Outside of this insane connection, the world was still moving at a rapid rate, gripped in fear of the unknown. COVID was circulating like a vulture over humans lying out in the savannah desert, slowly dying from the sun's extreme heat with no power to fight back. The reality was that, regardless of what was circling the perimeter and closing in on us unexpectedly, we were enjoying life. We were sharing great times, something that had escaped us for over thirteen years, which gave us a break from the immense routines of life that our jobs demanded from us.

At the time, only the power of four remained on the social media platform, after the fall of the famous six. They was completely unaware of what I was doing away from the power of four. I would never deem that to be an issue, as this power of four would never last in the long run. I was sure all four of us would return to a world of normality at some point, once lockdown and COVID-19 became distant memories. But separating the power of four would not be an easy separation. It would involve a process of fighting, arguing, and struggling for power from someone who could only be described as a narcissist, hell-bent on power, who only acted that way due to her unhappiness in life and in her own surroundings, and who always sought something more than just a Greggs. We had all come to desire things that were beyond our reaches during lockdown. In such situations, you really begin to value the things in life that you take for granted.

As the halfway point of the year rapidly closed in and the summer months approached, would we have an opportunity to enjoy the summer? Or would we continue to be locked-up animals, not permitted to face the outside world? We knew not what clearly existed outside and the associated risks, but the nation's people were slowly getting angrier at the situation, and braver in their quest to see family and friends. The rule breaking was very prevalent and open now; everyone could see it. Naturally, it would only get worse over the months ahead as the sun started to shine and society got brave and ambitious to seek that moment of respite after being locked in a cell that seemed no bigger than one's body and shrouded in darkness even when the sun shone through one's window. People in society would slowly, over time, start to turn on each other, as that is what we do when we face a war against an unknown source and don't know how to combat it.

It felt like we were doing a heist of the biggest bank in the world with a crew of eight, totally outnumbered by a source that we all feared. With no choice as to if or when things would not go to plan, the only option seemed to be to turn on each other. But when that heist came to a crunch point, we needed to unite as one unit and leave the bank with the greatest prize. We wanted to leave with the gold and ultimately our freedom. So, while we were now locked in the biggest bank in the world, how could we strategically plan to escape with the gold without being detected?

That was what life had become—we were involved in the deadliest of heists, where the chance of death was greater than the potential end reward. But we would go in armed for the unknown and take those risks to achieve supremacy and show that we were the resilient ones, with the cleverest plans to take down the bank and leave with the golden reward of freedom and a life that money cannot buy. I wanted to break into the bank and do a solo heist to achieve that supremacy. But the issue with achieving supremacy is you need to have skill, and my skill was still unknown to me. I appeared to have the skill of putting everyone else before myself, but that was a risky strategy, as it causes you to suffer at the hands of others. You can take a lion to a watering hole for a drink, but in all likelihood, if the lion wants a drink, it will plan to have the drink after it takes you out.

Chapter 7

TWENTY-FIVE SEVEN

*N*ow, for the toughest time that 2020 would bring for me, one that was unexpected by any stretch of my imagination. Even my naturally gifted sixth sense could not foresee how the month of July would end—sending me spiralling into a sense of grief and tragic circumstances that I would be powerless to stop. I desired a future I did not expect but kept at arm's length, not letting her get close enough to me for risk of breaking me all over again, as she had done thirteen years before when we woke one Saturday morning in a loving embrace.

· · · · · · · ● ○○○○○○○○○ ○ ○

Thirteen years earlier, as I turned over for a kiss and rose, I was the only one who knew that would be our final kiss this time round. I rolled out of bed and headed to switch on the kettle and turn on the oven to make our last supper together. With that done, I picked out what I would wear for our last supper, and I headed for the shower to wash the stain off my body after the night of passion that would very much be our last. Well, at least I thought it would be the last moment we spent together, in either my bed or hers for that matter. So, I had my shower and had a shave so that I looked my best for our last supper.

As I departed the shower robed in just my towel, she pulled me in close with sweet innocence on her face. And I could see her craving more of what we had been at just a few hours before. As she leant in to have that kiss, and to reignite a passionate embrace that would see us back in bed together, I knew that was not going to happen. I leant back from her kiss and embrace to release myself, saying, "Come on. There will always be later. I am so in need of coffee and a cigarette." So, I then headed to the kitchen, boiled that kettle once more, made us both a coffee, and then proceeded to get dressed.

Once I was dressed and she had showered, we both grabbed our coffees and headed outside for that morning ciggy. That was always the sweetest moment of any day, and the ideal chance to blow away the cobwebs of the night before. It was a beautiful morning, and we both just sat there in awe at the beauty on each other's faces. But then we finished and headed back indoors to have that breakfast, in no other than the style of the Irish.

So, I duly made the breakfast, and we sat down to eat and shared more coffee together. As we tucked into our breakfast, we talked about things that were slowly starting to get worse again. She had always had mental health sufferings, and with the best will in the world, she never did get any better and was a drain on me most days. It had come to the point that her direct refusal to get help was a daily chore rather than something I would embrace to get her some help and support her through these challenging times. And with that, I made the great announcement: "You must go."

There was shock and awe on her face as she sat at the other side of the table. As she opened her mouth to respond to the announcement, she kind of got tongue-tied, and tears started rolling down her face at what was about to happen. This was a moment of release in a way for us both, me knowing that it would go one of two ways: either she would now agree to go get help and we would get past this, or she would simply get up, pack her stuff, and go. She decided it was best that she went, so she finished her coffee, and we both ventured outside for a cigarette and sat watching the world pass by without a word to be said between us.

We both returned to my grotty little one-room bedsit to pack her stuff, and in a flash, she was gone—no kiss, no goodbye, no nothing, which was probably for the best, rather than leaving the possibility of a morning of tears and stress. But who would have known that in thirteen years' time, we would meet and rekindle our relationship and, on that occasion, I would be left broken and in tears, as if some sick revenge on her part to destroy me?

• • • • • • • • ● ○○○○○○○○ ○ ○

And now back to that period thirteen years later, when we rekindled that romance, which we had both believed would never happen. But there we were, very much together, as if we had been all along and never left each other's side. It is amazing how quickly time can pass, and this month went by so quickly. We spent nice days together whenever we could during that month. We had nice evenings walking along the beach hand in hand, like the break of the last thirteen years had never existed. I am sure neither of us anticipated what was going to happen as the end of the month grew closer and would bring something beyond thirteen years to a close, never to be returned to; holding that person in a warm embrace again would be like having to dig up a grave.

The events of twenty-five seven (25 July) brought our world crashing down. It was so bizarre that it was, of course, to happen on a Saturday. But the day had a much better feeling than that Saturday thirteen years before.

That Saturday morning went pretty much like the events of the drama we had experienced thirteen years before, but without the detaching and going our separate ways; that would not be known until the morning, in the sickest kind of fate. We woke very nicely cuddled up in bed. She had not been feeling great that week and had taken the week off work, but on that Saturday morning, she had a spring in her step that I had not seen in a long time. After a week of not feeling great, she seemed to be in very good spirits in many ways. So thoughts in my head started racing in a weird way. Was she pregnant? Hopefully not, as more kids was certainly something I did not want to have; having two beautiful kids was certainly enough to handle. Following the events that would unfold, it would have been great to have a child between us, but we knew we could never have kids together, which is why we never did.

On that morning, we thought of how nice it was to snuggle up in bed together, but we knew that we had to get up and moving, as she had to catch a flight back home that afternoon. So up we popped and shared a nice shower that time, and maybe got carried away while in the shower and afterwards as well. Who knew it would be the last time we had any sort of sexual contact between us, amazing as it was? With all that excitement, we clearly needed a shower to maybe cool ourselves off again, but we thought that might lead to only one thing, so we headed outside for a ciggy instead, with a nice mug of warm coffee. Outside, nicely huddled together in the summer sun, we enjoyed the moment. And she leant over and said, "You're going to make me one of your special breakfasts."

I replied jokingly, "Don't you think you had enough for breakfast this morning?" We laughed and laughed together, and with that, we went back up to the kitchen and got that fry-up on the go, proper Irish style, just as it had been thirteen years before. We sat down to eat with a glint in our eyes as we stared at each other across the table, and the conversation flowed between us nicely. She was so excited about getting to go home and see some family and friends. And to be honest, I could not wait until she left, as I knew the sooner she was gone, the sooner she would be back.

I got up to clear the breakfast plates and make two nice coffees while she grabbed her last few bits and got ready for the airport. Then, we sat outside in the summer sun, nicely snuggled together down at the bottom of the garden while enjoying a ciggy and drinking our coffee. And then we flitted up, grabbed her suitcase, jumped into the car, and headed off to the airport. As we drove to the airport, we had some tunes on. We were also laughing about the amazing experiences we had together over the past few months and joking about times in the past that we had shared together.

As we pulled up to the airport, we shared a very nice kiss and cuddle in the car before it was time for her to depart. The kiss and cuddle were very embracing; it felt almost as if it would be the last time, we shared any sort of intimacy between us, from what I can remember. And with that, she was rushing off with her suitcase dragging behind her, and me just watching in awe, wondering why we had ever departed each other all those years ago. She stopped and looked back with a cheeky grin, smiling like she never had before. I then pulled away in my car and headed back towards the M23 with the tunes up loud, sunglasses on, a good smile on my face, and a warm glow inside. I lit up a ciggy and wound down the window to catch the fresh July air.

When I got home, I bounced into the kitchen and whacked on the kettle, knowing how weird it was that as I went through the house, it would not be long before she touched down in our home country of Ireland, and she would see family and friends within the hour.

As soon as I had been in and had my coffee and a ciggy in the garden, *ping* went my phone. I opened the message, which read, "Just grabbed my luggage and going in search of my lift, missing you already."

I replied, "So missing you too and cannot wait to see you on Tuesday." And then I did not hear a peep out of her for hours, which was nice, as I knew she would be having a great time with friends and family, something that she had not done for months, with the whole lockdown situation and her high-profile job.

The night passed by so quickly as I lay and watched television. With the time getting on towards midnight, my phone pinged with a message; it was her. She said, "I am now in my bed, lying here dreaming of you, and wish you was here but I don't think I would be getting much sleep for a bit if you were here."

I replied, "Yes very much agree with that but how nice would that be. For sure gorgeous, when you get back on Tuesday, I will pick you up, and will start late on Wednesday and we can have a nice night together and a lazy morning together."

She replied, "That sounds amazing, cannot wait. Right, I better get some rest, or I may never get up in the morning. Night gorgeous."

And I messaged back, "Sleep well gorgeous."

The next morning being a Sunday, I decided to have a real lazy one, which was a normal weekend routine, with no need to get up and rush around. I knew she would do the same for hours, as no doubt, she had had a fair amount to drink the previous night. It must have been around 9am that I rose out of bed and stumbled to the kitchen for a large coffee and headed outside for a ciggy. By that time, I had already been up to have a quick ciggy before climbing into bed again and falling back asleep. Once I had my ciggy, I thought, *Damn, I have not even checked my phone yet,* and dashed upstairs to grab it from under my pillow and headed back outside and sparked up again.

When I got my phone out and unlocked it, I was like, *What the hell?* So many messages, calls, and voicemails from her friend, who had been ringing me nonstop since 6am. I had put my phone on silent mode so I could get a long, undisturbed sleep. I rang back her friend and said as she answered, "What's up?"

I could hear her crying as she tried to speak, muttering, "She is dead."

I replied, "Who is dead?"

She was crying. "She is dead! She is dead! She has taken an overdose, and when I woke this morning to her to see how she was, she just wouldn't move, and would not wake up."

I sat there non-responsive. As tears rolled down my face and my heart ached so bad, I thought, *What the hell is this?*

Is this a sick joke? All I could think of was that Saturday those thirteen years ago when I kicked her out like she was nothing to me and we had just had a one-night stand and no connection whatsoever. I thought this was the worst kind of vengeance she could serve to me, after I had treated her so badly only thirteen years ago. I was so distraught at the news and wanted nothing more than to just poison myself and join her in that place where we could be together, but I knew that was never going to happen, as I had to find a way to get through this. However, at the minute, my mind was just a completely blank space, apart from the pain!

And with that, I realised I was still on the phone. I hung up, stumbled back upstairs, climbed into bed, and just sobbed until I passed out.

Chapter 8

POWER OF SIX

As the trauma of the last few days had not quite sunk in, I was still reeling from the pain and trying to block it out in the best way I could. But that was never going to be easy. I tended to be quite open with everyone; however, this was the one thing that was just too much to bear, even with the people closest to me. I think my life was slipping into the darkest point it could ever get to and was so gripping that I totally started to close myself off from everyone like I had never done before. I do not recall even discussing this with my closest family members at the time. I was numb inside, with the horrors of what had happened. It still feels like some sick sort of justice that she had planned for me kicking her out all those years before.

It is mad how your powerful mind just creates stuff inside you that does not seem to be justified.

That month was as surreal as any other time of the year. Would that carousel of images ever stop spinning round and round? It would be great to get out of that circle of drama and travesty that just did not seem to stop. And this time, the cycle returned to the power of six, highlighting the society of hypocrites, who raised their heads again. Seriously, what is wrong with society and the conveyor belt of sick individuals who just cannot permit you to have a nice, peaceful life? To be respected was all that I asked for.

The power of six was such a struggle, and really, it was now just the power of four, since the two deserters were long gone. This time would certainly identify who out of the remaining power of four were the weirdest and most selfish individuals. It was mad to think the power of four was myself and three females but not the kind of foursome you would want to be associated with—and mad to think the females' names all began with the initial A. The worst of the group with the initial A always wanted to be the ringleader, but I was never one for being the leader, as I believe in self-value regardless of who anyone thinks they are. She was such a narcissistic person; she had a strange way of turning any situation to work in her favour. She did not realise the full extent of her behaviour, or else she just did not give a monkey, to be fair. I had the feeling that she was a twisted cow who was just interested in her own personal gain and would do anything to show that she was in control of everyone and could manipulate any situation that she wanted to.

I always was certain her behaviour derived from unhappiness in her own situation. She would turn on people and spread vicious rumours, then deny that she intended for them to fall like they did. And it was my turn. This was all off the back of the fact that I had started to speak to someone else, and this was totally not permitted by virtue of the power of four. I certainly must not have got that memo when we originally became the power of six. How dare I form a friendship with someone else outside the power of six and spend my days talking to someone else, so the jealousy had kicked in. What did she have to be jealous of? She had the perfect life with a husband, kids ... Or was the problem really that the rest of us were single and she wished she had that life?

She just assumed that something about a rumour that I was gay was true, and in true narcissistic style, she had to discuss it with other people. What about the chaos these things caused for other people? The other trauma I had in my head right then was enough to deal with. Why would she dare presume me to be gay, without maybe asking me the question directly to my face? We two had formed a good, strong bond within the power of six, and if she had just asked, then I would have quite happily answered her question. Clearly, I was not gay, and it had certainly never been an interest of mine. I was as straight as can be, but she thought the fact that I had been with different women that year was some sort of sick cover-up to hide my real sexual intentions. That would be a real sick way of treating people.

Yes, I did have a clear eye for women, and what was wrong with that? I may have been thirty-eight, but last time I checked, I was single and could do as I pleased when I pleased. And it was not like I was sleeping with many women all at the same time; trust me, one was enough to deal with. That spelt the end of the power of six (and the power of four), which would never be fully restored to what it had been when it all started earlier in 2020.

I was getting close to being done with the sick conveyor belt of bullshit around social media. There was enough sodden drama in the world without some sick, twisted, narcissistic crap, and all from one person who had the great habit of twisting everyone around her to sing to her tune at every turn. And I was very close to losing the plot, with the drama of only a few weeks prior, and with the added frustration of wanting to return home to Ireland to have a celebration of her life and scatter her ashes at our favourite location, where we had spent many a day together taking in the beauty of the South of Ireland. Ireland had such beauty, but no more than the beauty of the person I had spent time in it with. We will get that final moment together one day soon, when I can stand there, in our favourite location, and seize those minutes and think of the great times we shared together. As heartbreaking as that moment will be, it will weirdly be nice to be close to her one last time, before her ashes float off like a free spirit in the Irish sun.

Interestingly, some people really believe they are better than everyone else and brand this into others like their weapon of choice. In reality, no one is better than anyone else, and all they are doing is making complete idiots of themselves. That was very evident in the so-called leader of the power of six. She really believed she was so good that no one even came close to her in context. But, in fact, it was quite the opposite. She was just a loser based on her own unhappiness. It is sad that people need to act in such a way.

Her power struggles were very much based on her marriage not being what it needed to be anymore. I think everyone probably reaches this point, like the ten-year itch. She had grown attracted to other people and possibly even considered leaving her nice life to chase the dream of something fresh and new that a Greggs coffee and sausage roll could not fulfil.

When she first made a play for someone else, she used the power of six as some sort of cover for the fact that she was chatting with someone else and had an interest in them, and that was never going to work. I would never advocate for being used as a distraction tactic in any way in this situation. She seemed to settle, but sure, her husband had an idea as to what was going on and tried to unearth our association on social media at some point to break down the chain of events. I just did not anticipate it happening in the way it did. Thankfully, I did not bear witness to the night her social media vision came falling down around her.

She had ventured on holiday with her kids and husband, and one drunken night, she decided to do a live stream of her and her husband, who always heavily featured in the background of her live streams, like a bad penny that would just never leave. But on this occasion, he would become the centre of attention. They were apparently quite drunk. One thing led to another, and she got it all out on camera, and that was the end of that. For that moment of madness, her account was finished; her live streams got permanently banned as a result of the nature of the incident, and fairly deservedly as well. You could call this *karma* in a way; the right sort of karma was served to her, and her vision of social media came to a very damning end. The queen of the power of six had now been defeated all by herself.

Chapter 9

NEVER GOOD ENOUGH

*T*o date, the year 2020 had been a travesty of ups and downs, like the world's sickest roller coaster, and I was not quite sure how much more I could take of it. With every situation, regardless of how troublesome life gets, I really manage to find some silver lining. After the year so far, I was really convinced that it could not possibly get any worse. But as I say, every situation has a silver lining. Life is always going to be full of ups and downs; you just must run with it sometimes. And this time, it threw me an opportunity to try to move on all over again and restart.

I have always been a supportive person, and that good-natured approach never really changes. The issue with that is there are people in society who will always try to take advantage of good-natured people. Just as I was beginning to get back to a normal outlook on life in 2020, the next drama would be around the corner. *When is this year just going to be normal so that we can all go back to living like normal?* I really believe that the drama associated with the COVID-19 pandemic and the continuous issues derived from people not having a clue about what steps to take to manage the end of the current situation. It was a multiplication of sins, and the latest drama would be the direct result of influences at work, more hypocrites of society, and narcissistic people who like to take advantage of people's good nature. Sometimes, I really do not get the reality of the world that we live in, when so many people will stamp on and take advantage of good-natured people.

Work was going to be a real stress as we became the latest company to feel the effects of the COVID pandemic. In recent weeks, words to restructure had been sounding in our ears, and what that meant was clear: at some point, restructuring would be coming our way, as these things always work top down. And no doubt, with any employer, restructuring is when you discover how much you and what you have given to the business over the years are appreciated. But that aside, sometimes, restructuring gives you hope too as it throws at you some situations that you never imagined would resurface. In my case, it was as if this book flipped back to the very start, and my colleague who I dated for a short while appeared back on the scene. But this time, it was in a different context, as we both fought for our jobs.

Work's great idea to restructure the business came at the worst possible time for us employees, especially with the year we had had so far, with the management of the pandemic and the impact on the business. To be fair, the restructuring came as no surprise to me, as this business had never had a lot of respect for its employees, and this would show how it did not give a toss about us. In this situation, I would feel the biggest impact, but I was determined to make the right decisions by my morals, as regardless of anyone's opinion, I stand strongly by my morals and always aim to do right by them.

So, we pretty much were facing the reality of reapplying for our jobs, which is the most embarrassing treatment for any employee. And my opinion on this was expected: *As I approached nine years with the company, this was the reward—being reduced to applying for my job again, against external potential candidates as well? Where was the respect in that?*

This, in a way, reconnected me and my colleague, but that reconnection would not end well for us. Then again, the first time, it had not ended well for us either. How life does repeatedly spin round in the same circle. We had always had a good work connection and seen each other not as work colleagues but as good friends, but this scenario would see that friendship drift apart after the event had passed. So, for one last time, I got to help and support her, probably through the worst time we had faced together. Somehow, I knew she would be fine and would still have a job at the end of it, and probably, in a way, she needed it more than I did.

There were two possible job options on the table for everyone who was at risk of being made redundant. The option available to me was obvious, as you always go where your skill set lies. I had the option to step down and take on a store manager's role with a protected salary for two years, which was a very viable option for sure and one that I pondered for some time. And through the whole process, it was the one role I was hoping to get to not face the reality of being jobless in a matter of weeks. But then deep down, the reality was that I was unsure whether I would be retained within the business, as I certainly did not feel at home with the business as nine years of service approached. And towards the end, the reality started to kick in that I would not remain part of the business after all this time, and in truth, loyalty does not count in any shape or form. I clearly felt worthless to the business after every ounce of sweat, tears, and blood I had given to it since 2011.

Then the lightbulb moment hit: *Why am I lowering myself to take such an option that is so disrespectful and not about saving jobs?* The company chose to completely belittle us and put us in this position. So, from my stubborn stance, in the end, I was like, "No thanks," and made my decision to depart the business and see that part of my life behind me and move on. Every opportunity does present itself with an option to help someone who was stuck in a rut. But this was not so much the option, just another hypocrite and liar of society using their charm to get out of someone what they want from life, and as soon as they get what they want, they are gone. What is wrong with the scum of society, just expecting to take what they can get from the good-natured ones and not return what they are owed for the support?

Getting the redundancy money was a blessing, and I certainly have well used it and well kept it for future investment, but I shared part of it to give someone a new start in life, which she desperately needed to get her back on her feet. And regardless of the outcome to the situation, it was the right thing to do. We do not often have the chance to change someone's life for the better, but that does not give them the right to use it and disappear once they have what they want. The money gave this person and her son a new start in life; I was proud to have been able to support her and give her that new start, and I hoped she used it wisely. But as she took that opportunity to take without return, her karma would come, and here is some of it for you.

You do not take from the hand that feeds you where I come from. It is about moral respect. You can choose to ignore the situation and not return what you owe, but then, karma will come, as you will always have that on your conscience, and it will eat away at you like you have no idea. That will keep you awake at night like a bad nightmare, and you will remember it when you wake every morning.

You will have to look at yourself in the mirror and justify your life to you, of all people, and that is something you will be unable to do. When your son grows up, he will lack respect for you, as you will find yourself in the struggles of life and unable to dig yourself out someday. And you will sit and think of these moments of opportunity where you took complete advantage of some other person's good nature. Regardless of how much those moments initially improved your life at the time, your conscience will never recover from them.

Chapter 10

SUFFERING SEPTEMBER

September statistically has never been a good month for me, but it should be, as it is my birthday month. This would become the worst one ever, for sure.

My birthday is on 3 September, and I celebrated it alone with some self-love on the day, a new look, and some nice treats to try to perk myself up and get some motivation as the year just continued to take chunks out of my life. And this month would be no different from the rest, with me discovering how cruel and vile the social media world was over the month and the next few months for sure. The world of social media was full of amazing people I had met along the way, but social media also had a cruel part, and over the next few months, I would experience that like never before. It was really a society of haters and people hell-bent on destroying the great things people had achieved during what could be described as the hardest year most had ever endured. And this month brought trolling to my door, and it was personal.

I knew I had to be personal, as the trolls really sought me out at every opportunity, and not born of my reactions towards them. Towards the end of the month, the trolling would come to a definitive end that nearly ended my time on social media, which never really recovered. But with my stubborn determination, I fought back and remained in place, even after taking a heavy punishment for fighting back and defending my position in the world of social media. A vulture of jealousy was certainly beginning to circle back on the platform as well. This one was made up of jealous people just wanting to know everyone's business. And that was very vivid during this time.

Yet again, I crept off with someone on the platform for some fun. I never discussed her identity with anyone. They were unaware of who she was, but everyone was very keen to find out with who, when, how, and why all of this happened. This was not the first time we had shared in some fun over the year, and we had the right and privilege to do what we wanted when we wanted as grown adults. This time, we snuck off for a secret weekend in Skegness, much to the annoyance of many on the platform who were very nosily trying to find out who she was. But we were not giving anything away in this moment; we had not spoiled our few fun times together in any way. And that is not to say we did not drop any hints or diversion tactics to send people on the platform off the scent as to who we were.

We certainly had a great weekend in Skegness, which has always been one of my favourite holiday destinations in the UK, one that I am sure I will visit again and again. We enjoyed nice walks along the beach and visits to the arcades that were open. We enjoyed nice late nights in bed together and up-close-and-personal encounters, and nice mornings as well. We very much enjoyed lazy mornings snuggled up together, with the watchers on the platform very keen to watch our every move, like a very suspecting public spotting a celebrity. We spent the weekend throwing the odd curveball out there as well for them to feed on, as we kept her followers and mainly mine running around to our tune like in a game of cat and mouse, which we found really hilarious. And to this day, I do get asked a lot about who she is on the platform. We have kept it so still no one knows. Who knows? That may not have been the last time we endure in each other's company. But her identity remains only in my memory, and to my knowledge; it is the same with my identity amongst her friends.

On the Sunday, nicely cuddled up in each other's warmth, we enjoyed a very lazy morning with our own special breakfast on the menu. And then we had a nice shower together and nipped off for a nice walk along the beach before we went back to our cars to go our separate ways. Who knew when we would meet again for a weekend of fun, which it had always been for us? But there you go; in a nutshell, it was a great weekend, and still to this day, no one but her and I knows who she is. And that is the way it will remain for now, as there is nothing greater than the unknown. It is sometimes nice to share something with someone who nobody knows at all.

The rest of that month continued to throw ups and downs, highs and lows at every turning point. It just went from one extreme to another. Seriously, when would this conveyor belt of luck, or more so unluck, just stop so I could get off and stop spinning in my own drama? Or was this now exactly how my life was intended to be, just a roller coaster of events that would plunge my mind into continued darkness? It did make me wonder what we will think about life and how it all went when we all are lying on our deathbeds. I will probably be thinking, *I can get a permanent rest soon.*

As September closed, the drama just continued. But the next month was a quiet one, and to be fair, in many ways, I think I had had enough drama over the past nine months to cope with.

Chapter 11

FAMILY

*F*amily, for me, has always meant that you all stick together when it comes down to it. With every family, there always comes a time when the family members change and start to define themselves as individuals, get married, have kids, and build lives for themselves. And with that, the family drifts slightly in context, and the family members all tend to speak less. But when it comes to crunch times, you and your family should always unite, no matter what.

There are different kinds of families. There are the ones you are born into; in my eyes, when crunch times hit, these families always unite, regardless of the circumstances they face. Then there are families by association—the people you inherit over the years, and they become family, but in a different light. The world of social media, and especially the platform that I had commonly been associated with in many ways over the year, had linked me up with many families. And it really showed me how family can be overrated in many aspects. The core aspects of family were always there in every family I came into contact with on the platform. The fighting, the love, and the passion were there in every family in some context. It would be nice to have an easy life. But, then, that's not what family brings, is it?

I have four sisters, one brother, and a stepdad, who I absolutely treat as my own dad, as he has always been amazing to us in every way, and I have learnt so many great values from him along the way. And I cannot forget my mum, who has always been there for us through thick and thin, even though at times, we do not show the greatest gratitude for it.

On the platform, many families fought for position to prove they were better than everyone else, when, in fact, the reality is no one is better than anyone in this life. It does not matter how many people follow you on any platform whatsoever; you are only as good as the people who show you support and stand up for what you believe in. During that year, I had so stepped away from that and become a follower rather than a leader for my own ambitions, but over time, I would learn to feel again; someone needed to teach me that value. I was on a path of rediscovery in my life, and I was making the wrong mistakes time and time again, and this needed to stop. I needed to learn to value myself again and stop following the crowd.

Once upon a time, like in a fairy tale, I had really valued who I was, but as I stood and looked in the mirror, I realised that I no longer recognised myself for the person I had become. My foundational, core life values never left me, but I really changed over the year, kind of smothered the real person I was, and tried so hard to be something I was not. You just need to understand that the person you are is the great person, and those good things you want in life will come to you.

I was associated with many different families on the platform, and this was not a bad thing, but being associated with those families, I still felt I was trying to fit in, like some kid trying to fit into the society at school to avoid being bullied or picked on. On the platform, this was the case for almost everyone; we tried to fit into society in the toughest times we all faced.

In a way, it is amazing that fame always goes to people's heads in some way or another. Sometimes without you even realising it, it happens to you. The price of fame can mean that you just crush everyone who stood by you all the way and helped put you where you are today. When you achieve fame, you need to learn how to manage and show respect for everyone who supported you along the way. You need to define who is important and who is just there for themselves and doesn't care about the people who put you where you wanted to be in life. It really is such a travesty when people think they are better than everyone else and behave that way.

I first witnessed this with a family from the United States on the platform. I am not going to deny his values were initially good and the family had a good support network. We all valued him so much, with his positive approach towards everyone on the platform. But this family got kind of toxic, and it became time for me to depart. I was well settled being the follower, but I felt like my association with and work and energy in supporting the family leader, who I did have great respect for, had been overlooked and in a way disrespected. I became an outcast, and the final straw for me was when I witnessed a post by this person on the platform, which horrified me. How had this person, who I respected in many ways, changed and turned on someone who just did not deserve that kind of treatment, regardless of what they had done? So much for spreading love and positivity. For me, this family was done.

After departing all associations with this family, I felt for the others who had been associated in building support for this person and going on our great journey with the family, but it was time for me to break away and again focus on my own life journey and try to rediscover myself in some way. I was still struggling to do that. I had been struggling for some time, mainly since July, I guess. I was hiding how much I was still hurting from the events that had happened that month, which I still had not discussed in detail with anyone. I kept that pain bottled up inside.

It was heading towards November now, and a brief encounter led me to again make the stupid mistake of becoming a follower. Someone tracked me down, and they directly contacted me and wanted me to join their family. It was a big decision to make, as the last time I was associated with a family, it really did not go well. So why would this be any different?

As I lay and thought about the decision that night, I decided to go ahead with it. I had the feeling the situation would be different this time, as this person had sought me out, for they believed that I was a good person, and that was what they wanted the family to stand for.

Being part of the family was great in many ways, as the family instilled superb values in me in the early days and I fit in well. It was great to meet a number of amazing people, and being associated with this family was about to give me something and make me experience something that would define my life in a big way that I did not expect. The issue was it did not take long for things within this family to turn sour, with the leader of the family bringing it crashing down, based on their behaviour. It had barely begun, and the family really would have had length if it was not for the narcissistic behaviour of the person who set up the family.

It is amazing how quickly the glamour of fame can change a person. Or was it that the person had always been that way—they just wanted to develop a life that made them a better person? Either way, they were one of the worst people I had met in a very long time—a person who did not care for anyone around them in any way whatsoever. They saw everyone around them as minions in a factory that they could boss around at their leisure. And I had witnessed some disgusting things during night video call chats between the person and two others, so it did not take long for me to depart the family and be done.

The one good thing that came from my association with this family was the people. This family had some amazing people, and I made friends for life with them. I will value some of those truly inspirational people I met as amongst the greatest people I made friends with while on the platform in 2020. One person from the family definitely made me aspire to be a better person, and I really had no idea what was coming my way in terms of this person I had got to know and how they would soon shape my future. For so long, I had been longing to get myself back to being the person I was, having gritty determination and stubbornness and learning to live by my own life values.

It has been ever so hard to write this part of the book based on events that happened in the early part of 2021. I am writing this part of the book based on notes and the context of chats that I have had and the timeline of my life.

The reasons why this happened would become clear over the coming months.

Chapter 12

ISOLATION

You really would think as 2020 started to come to an end, there would be less drama, but that could not have been further from the truth. But then, what did I expect in the year where drama seemed to feed off me like tomorrow was never going to come?

The start of December was not too bad; I was just enjoying being back at work and having fun on the platform like I had the rest of the chill and relaxed times in the year—well, the few times when drama was not an issue. I had been working for an audit company since being made redundant in September, which was not too bad really. It kept me out of trouble while freelancing in cybercrime with the police to pass the rest of my time. But the end to the year was about to get very interesting. I would go through my third spell of isolation that year, and I had no idea it was about to bring a complete double whammy.

On 11 December 2020, I was assigned to do some work at a company in Tunbridge Wells, a place I was very familiar with from my previous job, in which I had managed three stores in the area over many years. While there, I really highlighted the stupid actions that some were carrying out and the risks that they were still taking. One employee had not been at work long one morning when he came down to say that his son was suspected as having COVID and he had to go home. I casually asked him, "Was you aware?" as he did look quite sheepish about it all. He did admit that he had suspected his son may have COVID. At that, my other colleague and I were like, "What the hell? Why would you be so naive to come to work and put us all at risk!"

At that point, there were no real concerns, as it was all just pretence; the colleague who was sent home was not COVID confirmed at that point. But amazingly, within twenty-four hours, it was complete chaos, with nine colleagues at that branch confirmed as having COVID. Then, my colleague and I were both off, as potential risks to the public. That was how the risk factor went. In a small, confined store, a total of twelve people were struck with COVID and made to self-isolate due to the naivety of one person.

I suppose you just must make the best of a challenging situation while locked away from society like some sort of prisoner. But I think we had just got used to it over the year. I suppose some of us were the lucky ones, who managed to get out of daily work and the element of social interaction it did give us. But there I was, back in solitary confinement, and I had no idea it would not be the last time that month it would happen.

December was such an interesting month, as it was the month that I wrote this book to keep me occupied during isolation. And it was the month that, at this point, I do not recall. I do not even remember writing the book. And yes, that may have you thinking, *What the hell!* All will become clear in further books, when I write about this month and why it is that I do not remember writing this.

Thankfully, as with the other occasions of self-isolation, I was tested and my results came back as COVID-free. I did have a theory suddenly. Could it be that certain people were immune to symptoms? Could it simply be that certain blood groups had immunity? I had that blood that could save everyone else's life, but they could not save mine. How could it be that with COVID looming, I could save someone's life, but if I took ill, they would be no help to me? Ironic it was in this world of craziness.

During the exciting part of that month, I grew to hate the family I was associated with on the platform day by day, and I would soon depart it in disgust at the leader's behaviour. At the same time, a certain someone in the family had caught my eye for sure, and I was keen to see if there was anything between us.

The isolation period came and passed so quickly, even though it did feel like a lifetime. In December, I was keen to spend some time with my kids in the run-up to Christmas. My ex-wife and I had debated who should have the kids over Christmas, and this was the one time I really put my foot down over it. So picked my two lovely kids up on 23 December and took them back to mine. We were barely through the door when my phone went, and it was the ex-wife. I was like, "What have I forgot?"

She was like, "Have you seen the email from the school? Our son has been in contact with a confirmed COVID case."

I was like, "Please tell me you are joking," which she was not. The excitement had so been real; now, I faced the reality that I was going to be self-isolating until the New Year at a minimum. What the hell was going on in this world? The year was clearly heading to a close in the cruellest way possible, with me being back in solitary confinement all over again. You know, they were bizarre times, with me being in complete isolation over the seasonal period. But I, being the person I was, did do a post on the platform in the lead-up to the big day, wishing that everyone who was alone this Xmas had a good Christmas and saying that I was only a message away, so they had no need to go it alone.

In a way, it was quite nice to celebrate Christmas Day alone, without all the demands of Christmas, where you must play all the games and have all the festivities and pretend that you are really enjoying it. The older you get, the more Xmas becomes a chore rather than something you enjoy, and the expense of it gets more ridiculous every year. However, the following week, I did a separate Christmas with my two amazing kids, and we had such a nice time. I supposed this was what it would be like every year going forward, with the kids having two Christmases.

That Christmas was a far cry from the Christmas before, when I had needed to pretend to enjoy Christmas even more. I am not going to deny I had a lot of fun during the period of isolation, and December was probably the best time I had that year. I felt good during that month, with not as much drama around, apart from being in solitary confinement all month. I was oblivious to the fact that in only a few months, being isolated would really shape my future in my darkest days.

As the new year drew in, I again had a lot of fun, with the new year about to bring something special to my door—something I had my eye on for a few weeks but was very apprehensive about. I wanted to learn from my past lesson. If I did get this opportunity, I wanted to make sure I approached it in the right way and hopefully not mess up again.

Chapter 13

GOING AGAINST THE GRAIN

*I*t is quite ironic that this book finishes on chapter 13, which is deemed an unlucky number. What better place to end the book than here, as the year 2020 was nothing but unlucky for me.

With the start of a new year, I was about to face the most defining moment of my life over the coming months. There comes a eureka moment in everyone's life, and I found mine just six weeks after the event of losing my memory and after weeks of pain, illness, anger, and frustration. At first, I thought losing my memory was all about the pain of chasing a memory that had simply slipped away. But it was so much more than that, and it would take over six weeks before that defining moment would come. This would be not just a defining moment of my darkest days but my life-defining moment, right there in front of me all along.

Life can be such a struggle, and after everything that happened in 2020, you would probably say that my memory loss was nothing in comparison. But for me, it was the darkest time of my life. I will not write about my memory loss at this point, as I will so in a future book. But I will say that everything in life happens for a reason, even tragic things. I really believe that your life is written and planned out for you, and how you react to every situation is what makes you a great person.

On 15 April 2021, I finally discovered my eureka moment (which I will write about in a future book). I had thought the situation that resulted in the loss of a year of my memory defined my moment, as it led me to discover the ability of writing. But that is not the case. And I have written two more books following up on this book, which I wrote in December 2020.

Because I wrote this book in December, I have no memory of writing it, which in a way is unique, as this book is my only link to the truth of what happened in 2020. It is the only thing I have that I can read and believe everything happened as I wrote it. It has been so hard to speak to people, some I do know personally and some I do not know but for our association through the experience of the past year. I have had to listen to people tell me stories of what happened over twelve months in my life and in a way completely take them at face value. It has been heartbreaking, as I have had to face some of the stuff twice over now, and even worse is the fear that if my memory does return the memories, I will have to relive them all over again. How the hell am I supposed to cope with living through a tough year, which I am not sure how I managed to survive the first time round and the second time, for maybe a third time? I am really starting to think that I would rather my memory not return.

And the weirdest thing is that I have fully rewritten this chapter based on the events of my eureka moment, and this is the only chapter in this book I have written from my heart and not from my head. The book has very much been a step-by-step story of my life over the past year, and I wrote it from my head. But this being my final chapter, it's written purely from the heart. And it has been such a difficult part to write, as I can only write most of it from a memory that I once had.

In life, it is so easy to let your head rule your heart, and we humans tend to never let our heart do the talking. If you let your head do the telling, you always go with the majority and the typical things; when someone does you wrong, you tend to lash out. I am no different from this stereotype: when someone does me wrong, I lash out. I have done that recently, but for the wrong reasons, and that is something I will have to live with for the rest of my life. We all have the option to step out and go against the grain and let our heart rule over our mind; we just choose not to take it, as logically, it just seems wrong.

In December, I met someone through the platform, and we initially struck up quite the friendship. Early on, our friendship was based on the actions of the family I was a member of at the time. It was down to the leader, and his behaviour with another member of the family, that our friendship first became apparent and that we both had a desire for something more than friendship. It would not be long before I decided to approach that leap of faith and take that risk to see where it would lead us both. It did take some consideration. But when I am certain about something, I do not leave it to chance in case the option may pass me by.

Our decision to take that step was one of great excitement and buzz; we had a great connection. During that experience, we both greatly understood each other and the situation that we were in—our lives outside the platform and the challenges we would have along the way. We were always of the same understanding, and we had great trust and respect for each other. The sexual attraction between us was very clear, but also, our connection was much more than that.

I've discovered that as you get older, it becomes very clear that you can change your dynamic and approach in everything you do. The key lesson you need to learn is that, as much as qualities already within yourself are what initially attract people to you, you must develop the quality of respecting people for the lives that they live and the circumstances that they have. When you reach a certain age, and once you have experienced certain things in life, you develop a better understanding of life's values.

For me, there are some things that I do not feel are right to express to the world. And as much as I am a person who is not ashamed to share my life experiences with those around me, writing and experiencing from the heart can sometimes be the hardest thing to do. This is because you hold your thoughts of the most sacred times of your life deep inside, and your mind controls what you share and do not share.

To put this in context in a way, your mind and your heart are the two major factors inside you that control you. The mind controls the thoughts and the memories you have in life. The mind is a very powerful thing, but without the heart, you never experience anything. In the science of life, you can survive and still function with a head injury. But if your heart stops, then you will no longer function. This is where my eureka moment came from, owing to that person who helped me rediscover what it is like to experience things from the heart. At that moment, I did not recall the last time I had felt something from the heart. I did not even recall when I had last determined what I felt from the heart and not from the mind.

My eureka moment came from the experience of being with the person and going against that grain of life experience that causes us to lash out and want to hurt someone back when something does not quite go as we had planned or expected it to based on the circumstances around it. We go through life always experiencing things every day; whether they be good or bad, they are all experiences. The things we experience in life cloud our future judgement of experiences, and we shy away from some things, as we feel history will repeat itself.

We frequently go with the grain in life and never against it because going with the grain seems like the only logical ideology. We expect it to help our minds ascertain the solutions to the problems that lie in front of us and what we are experiencing at the time. But the ideology is wrong. Going with the grain is felt from the mind; the mind is psychologically stronger than the heart, as that is the way it is designed. Your heart can have all the feelings, but the mind is what will control them. I gained my eureka moment from the reality that going against the grain is the ideology that we should all be following, not going with the grain. And with this, it is time to control the mind with the heart and feel things more. This moment purely came from the time I experienced with this person, and I believe that I never would have felt this way or learnt this very valuable life lesson if not purely for that one person who came into my life and allowed me to experience a different way of living. So, as I close out this book, I want you all to feel and experience how important this lesson is. And if you do not get it, then feel it rather than think it. I want those hypocrites of society as well, who again have been circulating like vultures, trying to tell me what to think and how to act, to stop. We cannot and should not act on the pretence of how other people think we should.

Naturally, there is nothing wrong with giving advice to someone, but if they choose to not act on the advice (not the approach you expect to be faced with), then that is where the conversation must end. Forcing your opinions onto others and showing disgust when they do not follow your advice is an issue. In my case, the experiences I shared with that person meant a lot to me, and all because I decided not to take the relevant treatment, I thought I deserved the ideology of going with the grain; and I have to live with that choice. But understand this: ultimately going against the grain was my choice, and it was not one that came from the mind; it came from the heart.

Then, I decided to go against the grain and show that

person the support they needed regardless of the decision they made, as it is easier to cast someone to the memory of life rather than to be the bigger person and be there for them when they need it the most. And they may not even know that they need it, but sometimes, we all need someone to watch over us and check on us regardless of the outcome, with us not expecting anything in return.

You earn value in life by doing great things, especially when you expect nothing in return. I have never regretted anything in my life up until recently, and I will carry that one regret with me to my grave, but it is that one moment of madness—disrespect—that defined my eureka moment. And if it was not for the person who allowed me to experience their life and how they lived it, then I would have never had the opportunity to become the person I am today. And I will always hold this person in high regard, as they are an amazing person, and they deserve the respect that going against the grain brings.

About the Author

Kian Ireland grew up on the streets of Belfast, Ireland, and has lived in southeast England since 2007. He has two amazing children, five siblings, five nieces, and one nephew. He has two fantastic parents who could not have given him a better start in life.